GETTING WITH THE FLOW

HOW TO
IMPROVE LIFE SKILLS

PRANSHU CHANDRA

Liber
Media & Designing

Liber Media & Designing

Genre : Self-Help
Edition : Paperback

Copyright © 2024 Pranshu Chandra

Published by Liber Media & Designing

THANK YOU TO CHOOSING FLOW

"THERE IS A LITTLE PART OF OUR HAPPINESS AND JOY"

ABOUT THE BOOK

GETTING WITH THE FLOW IS A SHORT PHILOSOPHY OF LIFE. IT IS DESIGN TO IMPROVE SOME LIFE SKILLS. IN THIS MOMENT WE MAKE A HAPPY OR JOYFUL LIFE.

THE PURPOSE OF THIS BOOK IS TO PROVIDE SUCH A PERSPECTIVE ON LIFE THAT CAN AWAKEN THE ABILITY TO DO EVERYTHING AND THE DESIRE TO DO SOMETHING BIG.

WE ARE CAUGHT BETWEEN MANY THINGS IN LIFE. WE DO NOT KNOW WHAT IS THE RIGHT DECISION, WHY LIFE SEEMS EMPTY, DISCUSSION OF SOME KNOWLEDGE, SOME SOCIAL, SOME ECONOMIC AND SOME EDUCATIONAL ISSUES ETC.

AS YOU CONTINUE YOUR JOURNEY, YOU SHOULD ALSO THINK BIG BECAUSE WE HAVE TO DO THIS WORK FOR FREEDOM.

GETTING WITH THE FLOW

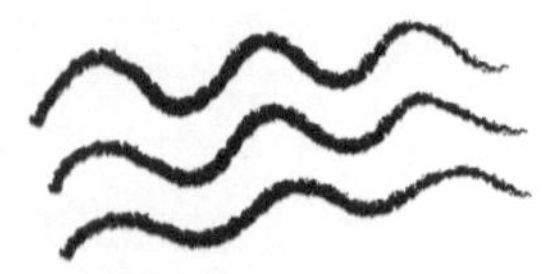

CONTENTS

Introduction-

- Learn to Say any Conversation
- Read Books of Successful People
- Failure and Experience
- Habit of Negotiation
- Management of Pleasure
- Power of Thoughts
- Goal Achievement Process
- How to Live Peacefully?

Conclusion-

• • • • • • • • • • • • • • •

Introduction-

When we want a state of happiness in life and we also want a peaceful life, then flow is the only thing with which we can achieve happiness. The ups and downs in life make us wonder what the outcome will be or why something isn't working out.

With the change of times we are so busy with technology that the goal is to build the ability to experience a juice-filled life. Our environment can take us to a very high state of peace but we also have to make efforts in this. We have to give our priority only to those things which strengthen the spirit of sacrifice and make it meaningful.

The key to peace is to connect with the present or go with the flow. There can be accuracy in our actions only when we remain focused in an environment that has flourished through our labor and struggle.

We have to reach a mental state of renunciation. Only then will sacrifice be ignited in the inner thoughts and everyone can do some noble and cooperative work. Keeping this feeling in mind, the author is publishing some important philosophies through his thoughts.

All of them are aimed towards a single goal that can lead to greater heights, as opposed to a boring life. Everyone should try to do something unique according to the current situation.

Where life tells us what things should get priority first. It could be peace, freedom, knowledge, economic goals etc.

Enjoying nature is truly a unique moment. What a sound, a tone, a rumble, absolutely in tune.

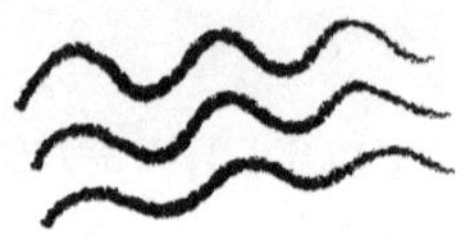

Role of Time Management

Who can stop the dogs? I don't know why they bark. So can we stop them? Life is also like this. Time keeps passing by so can we stop time? We have always been learning something new, doing something new, achieving something new. In this developing life everyone is running, can we stop the running. not at all.

If time is not available then don't do it. Look! The question is not how we manage time. The question is how do we organize the work. We will not be serious about this matter. We'll just know how to get the job done. Because only work can organize time.

First of all you should know where the time is being spent. If we do not know the functions of time then how can we know time. For this you have to be precise.

We know that every drop fills the pot. Then it has to be understood that time will not be arranged suddenly but gradually or with continuous efforts.

"With good habits and focus on work, time is never wasted"

Great philosophers explain that meaningless work does not yield any benefit nor does time get organized, but unnecessary energy definitely gets wasted.

"If a task seems difficult then it should be divided into pieces, otherwise the task will seem bigger"
The best thing here is that human thinking also has solutions to problems. Due to which the state of life can be arranged naturally.
Avoid doing useless tasks. Yes, one thing must be remembered that before starting any work, we must think once whether it will be right to do it or not.
"One does not get the opportunity to achieve great heights in life again and again. But we must have faith that we may get another chance"

Every Person is Equal

No matter how we feel. But everyone here is working. Here everyone has equal time. Everyone's work is good. Everyone can do something big.

"But the difference between successful and unsuccessful people is that successful people keep learning something or the other"

Every person can achieve everything in life if he has the confidence to learn everything. Try to understand everyone's problems and situations.

When someone says "I can't do something" because I'm different. He thinks and says this completely wrong.

But if he looks at every person with equal respect and tries to learn something from them, talk to them, read, listen and watch them. So that person will never be able to say that "I am different and can't do anything".

Goals and Task Importance

What makes the goal bigger? Only the work makes the goal bigger. After all, what is the goal? That is the complete form of the work. Don't look at life as a goal. Having goals in life means goals are created within life.

Life is a journey in which we travel between happiness and sorrow. Goals are part of life. It is a complete work. When we set a goal then our work also starts.

Think once before making a goal and do not find it necessary to change it after setting the goal. If the target remains accurate then there will be improvement in the work and efficiency of the work will increase and there will be no interruptions in work.

"Goal is the part of life which provides constant motivation to acquire efficient knowledge in life"

The smallest tasks that happen on a day-to-day basis are tasks. Accomplishing tasks saves us time and provides constant happiness.

It is very important to have daily tasks in life so that our morale and efficiency increases and we are ready to solve the challenges that come ahead and keep learning something from them.

It is not difficult to give a right goal to life. The goal should be determined according to your expertise and interest.

The goal should be such that, we all keep learning something new among human beings.

The goal may take more labor and more years, it may also take a few months, the goal may also be accomplished in less days.

"It should be accepted that the obstacles that are coming have come only after setting the goal, hence there will be a solution"

No one has lived or can live without work. Make your work the most fun, engaging and quality. A unique time will definitely come which will accelerate the pace of everyone's goals.

Sometimes the goal is accomplished without us even realizing it. This happens with those who never set goals.

They make their work their goal or assume that this work is their goal. In such a situation, he has nothing to do because he is preparing for a big goal without even setting a goal, his work is the highest and is full of wisdom.

Role of Attraction in Life

Sometimes it happens with us that we want to do something but we postpone it. We have full strength to do that work also. But I don't know why we don't do that?

Do we know what is happening to us? Or what are we doing? Everyone's intelligence is different but the qualities are the same, the tasks are the same. From now on, we will stop the habit of procrastinating and do the work which is right. Without attraction the goal cannot be accomplished. Meaning to say – if attractions are happening then do not leave them. They are part of or included in the goal.

"Forget the fear and explore the attraction more deeply"

Then suddenly all the confusions and mistakes in the goal will automatically start getting corrected and one will enter the successful path. You have no limits. The goal is not achieved by living within limits because our goals are unlimited.

"Success is tasted only among successful people"

Life-Line of Successful Personality

There is a line in the life of successful people, which is called accuracy. Life is a confluence of ideas. If we look at the state of thoughts in life, we will find that our attraction is mostly on those habits which are the needs of every person's personal life.

Life can be improved by changing the life line. One wise man is greater than a thousand fools because he is conscious. He knows what he is. He can do anything if he wants.

Is there such a thing as changing the life line? Of course, the lifeline is accuracy of knowledge. Life lines are thoughts and thoughts are actions.

We can change life by changing thoughts. We can definitely bring about change by acting wisely.

Every person should understand that the future is completely in his hands. The future can be won by removing fear. One who has the future in his hands cannot be anyone's slave.

We have a lust to acquire various things and the life line is the opposite of all this. She completely resists fear.

"Just as without food one cannot fill one's stomach and one cannot gain energy, in the same way fear does not go away without knowledge"

Knowledge is the only source of wisdom. Without knowledge, one cannot become wise or there is no question of changing the life line.

"Try to remember once again that the lifeline is 'ideas'"

Remember that a successful personality is the same in personal life and professional life and is not artificial.

It uses clothes to cover the body, food to energy the body and knowledge to develop the society.

A unique life full of possibilities. You have to make a significant effort to gather knowledge. The feeling of lust is corrupt. Be careful!

✦

Role of An Ideal

An idealist is a person dependent on ideals. He becomes successful in his journey by considering a successful person as his ideal.

He understands the importance of his ideal. He knows the experience of his ideal.

"Good people are worth more than 1000 good books"

When you don't understand what, something and why? Then understanding the importance of Guru is equivalent to reaching heights.

In the fast pace of time, an ideal person is necessary who keeps inspiring. The credit for which should go to the Guru so that he can make our efforts more successful. Guru or ideal cannot be compared with anyone. Whatever is said about them is very little or nothing at all. The position of Guru is the highest, without Guru knowledge is not attained. Guru enjoys the highest status among all Gods.

Problem Solving Method

Some of our stupidities lead to big problems. We fool ourselves in every field. The problem is not as big as we think. Problems arise due to lack of education. To control problems, thinking has to be controlled. We can find solutions to all problems not by controlling our thinking but by developing right thinking.

The biggest problem is of thinking. We start reducing the joy of life by thinking about problems which is not right. Face the problem with some other problem and the solution to the problem will definitely be found.

Be happy even when you feel problems because problems are also unique and teach something. Regarding money, she says to spend it at the right place, regarding studies, she says to read good books.

"Use why questions in a problem. If there is a problem then why is there, if so then why is that" Different problems in different areas, but life is joyful. Keep doing something in life, work according to your priority. Better actions lead to better results. No information can be obtained without reading a book, in the same way one cannot get the solution by talking about the problem.

News-Paper Reading Role in Life

We get new information, new inspiration, free thinking from newspapers only. Something new on every page, an easy way to understand information. However, when technology was not in vogue, information about exams was available in newspapers only.

In modernity, we have replaced newspapers with phones, which is wrong. We have lost our patience. As if we want to do any work very quickly. Have lost your peace.

Some pages in the newspaper give information about the surroundings, some about the country and abroad, some about literature. The time is also not being utilized properly because there is no discipline. But discipline has to be learned from the person who comes to deliver the newspaper, he comes on time to deliver the newspaper, be it winter or rain.

We also started using newspapers very less. We have to give some juice to our life again. We will have to discuss the news among ourselves. You have to discipline your daily routine with discipline.

"We have to analyze what is good"

Money Management Role in Life

After filling life with all the skills, the most important thing is the management of money. With time our expenses have become uncontrolled which pushes us into the category of loss. When do we realize that the money we have is being used in wrong places - wrong clothes, wrong food, wrong things.

Sometimes we let money go so out of control that we start considering it a problem. Our analysis is so low that we do not react even after knowing all the expenses, just think about the same even when it is not spent. It is immaturity to unnecessarily demand or spend on services that are not really needed.

We consider our knowledge superior and if someone tells us something new then we have no time to tell ours. Will money be managed like this? If we say that money is not everything then we agree. If we don't try to save anything. Everyone will have to make efforts for good health and good services.

"Spending everything is worth it if the place is right. Find the right place"

Effect of Circumstances

Human nature is also strange, it adapts to every situation, most of the people try to adapt themselves. The right thing would be either to leave everyone behind and move forward or to take everyone along and work without discrimination and move forward.

We like everything, we don't like any one place or any one thing. We always demand something new. Is man meant to live a life devoid of any kind of education?

For example, if someone whose job is to run machines, instead of paying attention to the machines, he focuses on others and someone else controls the machine, then can he control the machine? One who likes any work should not do it because that work can also be wrong. In this example, one does not get anything by working against the circumstances. Neither will we learn anything nor get educated.

The same thing applies to the situation that if someone has to be taught something then he will have to be given a situation only then something new will happen. Everyone's views are opposite to each other. Some speak according to experiences and others speak according to circumstances.

"Experience teaches that if you can quench someone's thirst, then quenching it means not holding back from helping"

Life breaks a lot and then we leave something behind and constantly try to move forward. It is believed that disease also attacks the weak. The job of the brave is to fight. We become very objective in life when we realize what is real then we become humble.

Changing your lifestyle and finding the right lifestyle is a matter of circumstances. Stomach pain also occurs only when we eat something wrong, otherwise there are many life-giving substances.

Our choices challenge the circumstances. If we choose that it is very difficult then nothing will happen, whereas if our choice is right then it means that I will not be able to do it, then what is the point of trying.

"To surrender without facing circumstances will never make one great"

Truth doesn't scare you, circumstances always scare you. Similarly, life does not run through imagination, it runs through action, work and duty. We need inspiration to move forward. It is not foolish to say that any situation is right without knowing it.

"The purpose in life will be right only when the circumstances are right. If the circumstances are wrong then there will be wrong objectives"

We need to change the scene, the people themselves will change, right education is needed. False devotion does not work, power does.

Only when that glimpse is visible or gets to be seen should it be accepted that there is some change in the circumstances. The feeling and imagination will happen automatically. There is no danger in proper education; the question of justice is discussed with the Guru.

"One who is humble, circumstances do not affect him"

There is no fear of losing anything. Because there is fairness, compassion, a vision of justice and unlimited willpower.

What should not Want?

We are not meant to keep anything for ourselves. We should not keep anything with us that will prevent us from helping others. For example, instead of throwing or burning old clothes that you have, giving them to someone in need is the highest state.

"The aim should be to work without noise"

To make life wonderful we have to sacrifice many things which we have in vain. Would we ever want to give the leftover food to someone who really wants it?

It is a great desire to bring life to an easier state. If any desire is bigger than this then it is greed and useless. We will have to give up the desire to receive and work on giving, then the easy state will start appearing on its own.

Art and Music Culture

Both art and music are admirable. The gift of art and music is to fill life with joy. It can be made from any object and sound. It is unlike any attraction. It provides happiness in many ways.

The feeling of art and music is a sign of consciousness and understanding. The entire universe is moving and in motion with art and music. Its essence is included in every part of it. Everyone will have to be interested in art and music, only then peace and favorable environment can be created.

"Art and music are the two most beautiful parts of life"

Every person gets to experience art within himself. When art is encouraged and respected with bravery and courage, then no one will be able to stop it from developing and making the nation attractive.

"Art and music are natural things which make human life enchanting"

Importance of Decisions

We try to participate in any decision. We need to know what is it keeping in mind how we can take the right decision and what is its importance, how does it play a role in success. Together we will look at it from a different perspective.

First of all we have to leave behind greed, remove our wrong desires, only then we will know about it in detail, then we will have to take care of human welfare and safety.

How do we know that this decision is right? Right decisions cannot put us in any trouble. Suppose five people are hungry, you are also one of them and you have fifty rupees. Now you distribute ten rupees among everyone, ten to yourself and ten to everyone else. Then your decision is right, your viewpoint is absolutely right.

There are many such examples which always help in taking right perspective, right decisions. If you also had the same viewpoint then good luck to you.

Now how will we understand its importance? Its importance is that we did the right work in a short time. Many tasks were also completed, there was no fear of anyone, there was nothing to worry about.

"Life is yours, the only fair decision made from your soul is the right one"

Keep a Small Diary

With speed, some things have to be kept in mind with precision, some things have to be remembered. Tasks, some important work, expenses etc. In this hectic pace, it will be necessary for us to spend some time on paper work instead of technology.

It would be right for us to know that after all the important work that we do by using diary can be done easily with its help.

"List making is an art, a tool for success"

When we step back a little from technology, we will find that our thoughts are getting a foundation of purity and strength. Technology has its place. Many of us do not use technology properly. Writing a few words on time maintains the purity of thoughts.

We have to write tasks in the diary and rapidly improve ourselves and the quality of our work so that others can do better work.

Be Aware and Focused

Doing something to solve the obstacles in your goal makes the goal stronger. One who works in any field in an alert state and moves ahead.

"Awareness is finding opportunity in difficulty"

It will not be enough to be alert in any work, rather we will have to develop the ability to understand it and what its philosophy is. This cannot be said in any one or every area of life.

Just as there is no darkness in light and there is a need for light in darkness. Similarly, how to do the work with good performance is awareness. Awareness is revealed in difficulties.

Like you don't have information about anything, let's say about any transaction. Then you will either make a loss or you will miscalculate. Here we came to know that we cannot do any good work in the absence of information. Vigilance is acting according to the knowledge of the tasks.

Now how to work from the center or how to bring concentration. Leave aside all the useless things and try to contribute to one cause. Any time can be appropriate here.

Once upon a time, a man was planting fruits on his cart. Some people came to ask him whether anyone had gone through this route, but he denied that he did not know.

He was so engrossed in his work that he didn't even realize that ten trucks had passed by and the road had started shaking. There was no one around him, everyone had run away. This is to do the work with concentration.

In this context we do not even know who is doing what, what is happening where. Life is also like this. Whatever happens, we should not be deprived of information about our goals.

"Better attention is the result of better information"

There is so much difference between awareness and meditation that awareness is a means of making the outside things good and meditation is a means of making the things inside.

When you are walking on the road, watching your path is awareness. You are walking on the road, you have to go where you want to go, there is concentration there, that is the goal.

What is Costly?

Once upon a time, four friends lived in a house. There was friendship among all four. But sometimes they used to quarrel among themselves, two of them wanted to go out somewhere, the other two friends refused to go, both of them said that it was better to keep doing something here rather than going out.

One day those two friends who wanted to go out ran away without informing the other two. When they found out that both of them were not there, they said among themselves that we should have gone with them, should have accepted their advice.

Then they say that we will also go out because nothing is looking good here. They also went out for a walk and the group of friends parted ways, never to meet again.

Here we came to know that we should never sacrifice freedom for any place or thing because freedom provides novelty and happiness.

By staying at one place, we stop liking that place and we get bored. Everyone desires freedom, it seems that no one and nothing is important, meaning freedom is important. Due to living in freedom, there is a desire to do something new.

"Freedom is precious and valuable"

"Nothing in life has more importance than freedom"
We learned how important freedom is in life. We should know how it works in success.
"What do you do when you're at home, what do you do when you're in the office"
How will you set a new and bigger goal if you remain engrossed in things? Similarly, when you have a goal then only you will work on it.
"The body tires of laziness, not of freedom"
Everyone wants freedom, so how can we get it? Freedom is not achieved by achieving something, it is achieved by leaving something. Accomplishing all the goals before the stipulated time is a sign of freedom which will make life more fulfilling and complete.

———————❖———————

Solid Perseverance

What is the quality of solid work? The answer to this question is very short. For example, you have an exam tomorrow. Five questions are asked in it. The time is twenty minutes. Now you spend all the time on one question then you will not be able to complete the questions and your marks will be less. You have asked two questions. Till now your marks are twenty. To be successful you have to get fifty out of fifty marks. You have to finish each question in four minutes, only then you will be successful.

Where is the solidity in this? Success marks are fifty and questions are also five. Then spending four minutes on each or solving one question in four minutes is solid work.

You did high quality work within time, this is called accuracy and given limited time on a target, this is called perseverance. You did everything, this is called solid.

Good Habit Patience

Is patience necessary? Not at all, because when something like a goal is in front of us then why should we not achieve it. There is a pen in front, why should we ask for it from anyone, why should we go to the shop to buy it. Then where is patience necessary? After trying, patience is necessary until what is desired is achieved.

"Work is patience, work is energy, work is results" Is it like that? It's just that when you decide to do something, you have patience, no, you do it, and you do it consistently. Work is important, so why not have patience at all. Patience is also work. Work is the result. If you want better results, you will have to work better.

There is definitely laziness, there is no patience. If someone says or listens to patience somewhere, then he is saying do not be lazy at all, do not waste time in laziness.

"Get up, stand up and try until you succeed"

Rules and Discipline

There are no rules in life but there are plenty of rules in actions. Rules to make the work higher and bigger, rules to complete the work, rules to learn from work.

Daily activities are carried out following certain rules. Some are complete and some remain incomplete. What are the rules? Rules are a map. Do not go out of this map, work has to be done within this map only, go to the places present in the map only.

"Preparing a map is a rule and preparing a map every day, every moment is a discipline"

"Some rules are economic, some social and some at the educational level"

No rule exists, either the rule is of experience or of knowledge. What is knowledge and experience? Knowledge inspires to do something new, does something new. Experience makes work stronger and experience comes with knowledge.

Discipline is the strength of rules. The stronger the rules (no matter in which field), the stronger will be the discipline. So what is discipline, strength and whose rules?

Rules are prepared through knowledge and rules are collected and discipline is formed. It is seen which has more importance in achieving the goal. So that's about discipline. Living amidst discipline gives one security. Which completes the map in the right direction.

In discipline work, there is one word, let's say that word is 'Nature'. You have to remember this word. You will remember it in two or four times or in one go.

"Only if there is a group of words will there be need for discipline"

Don't limit it to just words. This is an example. The effort is that strength is needed, then discipline is needed. See, here there is governance in discipline and governance means strength. Without rules, discipline will be of no use and rules are made from knowledge.

"Knowledge is meaningful in all aspects"

Reading and Writing Method

If something is truly important then it is the process. Labor and knowledge are two things necessary to complete any work. So what is this process? For once, link writing with labor and link studies with knowledge. We don't need to do anything more here.

"Knowledge and hard work are the real keys to success"

When this is revealed then everyone is surprised so that we could know about it in more detail. But time is also strange, when it realizes then time also says that there is still time.

"One's circumstances can be improved by knowledge and hard work"

If a human being has the greatest gift, it is that of writing and reading. Can any animal do it? Think and speak.

The treasure which we search for everywhere, is not present anywhere else but here. It is a treasure to be expanded, firstly of studies and secondly of writing.

Health Management

We will never believe that we do not believe in the one who can change everything. Believe in what does not change. Here it is about health. We take advice from anyone for even the smallest things, isn't it harmful? There are many ways that help us when we feel free. It is difficult to believe that one can become healthy even through knowledge.

Health also has some values. For example, when our health is good then we do not pay attention by eating wrongly. You have full power to make you feel that this is unnecessary for me. When you get stuck in the same topic you are talking about, the talk is not important. What is important is a big goal.

What if the weather changes, the place changes? But the goal should not change, this is health. There is no point in talking about small things and small topics.

"Labor and knowledge are health, fulfilling which is the responsibility"

Learn to Say any Conversation

Why is dialogue important? If I ask what is necessary in work and conversation then both are necessary but when we know what is appropriate then we can move the work forward by talking once.

We don't have to get stuck in the middle of a conversation. There is something beyond conversation that is very polite. The only difference is that we give more importance and time to conversations than actions.

"Language is the foundation of communication, strong language is necessary"

It is necessary for humans to learn anything. As many subjects as there are, for all at any level. It's hard to do well without talking. But here is a solution.

That level does not oppose anyone. It strengthens the sense of knowledge. It is prohibited to discuss certain issues that may hurt any person. Such topics are completely prohibited.

The purpose of language is agreement. When a person is talking linguistically then he is compromising and entertaining at the most.

"Success is achieved by action, not by compromise"

Read Books of Successful People

Books of successful people teach something new. The topic of each is selected by dedicating it to its readers or they provide guidance by taking the work forward.

There are books on many subjects in the world of books but if we want success then we should not stay away from reading books of successful people.

Life is developing. Most books have tried to develop it. Today, crores of autobiographies, novels and various types of self-help literature of successful people exist.

Which gives very accurate and practical information about management. The law of attraction is related to books.

Ultimately it can be said that there are some unique people. His work is guidance because no one should fail, that is why he makes books the path of guidance.

"Reading books strengthens development"

Failure and Experience

When the path seems clear, we learn only so much and gain very little experience.

"If you learn something from failure, that is experience"

We do not want to learn everything in life because our failure is clearly visible due to discrimination. We should never want anyone to fail, we want experience.

We can fail only when we consider something as success. If we believe that success and failure are nothing or words then our concentration will be on our work and success is achieved as soon as the work is completed. What is learned from obstacles in work is experience and failure.

"Achieving or not achieving something is not success/failure"

Some make a temple a home, some make a temple in their house. It is for the one who considers success. If anyone says what is success? So success is an experience. The experience gained after failure is a strong experience. After being successful, one experiences success and after failure, one experiences failure.

Habit of Negotiation

Perspective:

(i) Hey! My marks were only fifty out of hundred. Come on, at least we passed, no problem.

(ii) How did I get such low marks despite so much hard work?

Have you seen the difference between these two viewpoints?

One says passed, he stops. The other one says, hey my marks are so low. How can I get such low marks? How?

It is right to ask this question. This cannot be kept in the category of compromise.

Our attitude determines our success. He tells in advance whether we are waiting or doing something. The one who compromised has stayed. This is the one who does not succeed by making compromises, he is stagnant and has no desire to increase his knowledge.

The habit of compromise is the path to failure. One who compromises on every matter cannot work hard. At the same time, I will work hard again, I will keep finding the answer to this question. I will learn and find out how it can be done.

"Compromise is a sign of a weak personality"

Management of Pleasure

It is said that the feeling of satisfaction is called happiness or happiness, so are we ever satisfied or are we ever happy? There may be some way to arrange happiness or joy.

If a desire emerges when we are satisfied then it is satisfaction but not a desire to get something or to give something. Our happiness flows from the fact that we establish our work with full dedication and with the right relationship, with a spirit of giving.

If there is happiness without getting hurt then it is deception. Many relationships in life that we maintain, it seems that everyone is satisfied but it is not so. To do something different from people, to do something new, to do something that no one around has done or is about to do.

You do that work in a different way with speed and flow like you do everything with pre-planning. We realize what we will do and what its consequences will be. If we do not know the consequences, will we do anything?

"Only great struggle is true satisfaction without deception"

Power of Thoughts

There have been works about the unique power of thoughts that can do something that no one has done before. The discoveries made in the field of science till date show us something different as if something has happened due to some flow.

The world is something special, something different. How many ideas are there in this? The consequences of some thoughts are associated with goodness. When we look at life from its perspective then we see something different. When we forget ourselves and look at ourselves then we look different.

Are whatever results have come till date the result of ideas? Are we playing with words? Is it okay to fill life with thoughts? How time and thoughts go together in our environment. When questions arise in these thoughts again and again. Then something infinite happens. We get solutions to every problem and problem which we do not want.

Our unlimited store of thoughts makes us do something unique. As a result of which we can bring many things under our control. When someone thinks about a task, he completes the task and gets results.

Is what we call truth only a thought?

What will happen if we do something that leads to the truth? Everyone wants a good life and wants to live life in the right way. Some are going to gain a foothold in some field and some in something else unique. Someone wants to know something.

What is the language of our thoughts? According to me, the first is 'imagination' and the second is 'dream'.

Life can be changed by one thought. When nothing external comes into play in life then only thoughts come. When a person's emotions are in a state of love, then thoughts also work in a different direction.

Once upon a time. There lived a group of fishes in a pond. A very big fish also lived in the same pond. Some other creatures also lived in the pond. The big fish thought that I had to protect all this. One day the fish thought why should I protect them? When the big fish changed its mind, it ate some of the fish. Some remaining fish think that how did it eat everyone, it used to protect everyone. She thought about it but forgot to leave that pond. You will know what happened next. The remaining fishes also could not do anything because they wasted time in thinking and thought wrongly. If she had thought of going away from there, perhaps she too would have been saved.

Many people do not know the truth. Despite being entangled in thoughts, the truth is not known. Because they think but not in the right direction.

Many of our tasks have stopped because of thoughts, we will be surprised to know that this is the power of thoughts. All our thoughts are wrong until we are stuck in a situation.

Life is unique fill it with unique and strong thoughts. Do we know why someone is rich, knowledgeable, lazy or a thief? From your thoughts. That is why it is said that thought is behavior.

What is it about thoughts that changes everything in an instant? What we see, what we hear, what we do comes from our thoughts. If someone is unhappy with thoughts, he is happy with thoughts.

Those who are great do not do anything different. Someone's words cannot be called wrong as long as his thoughts are pure. Purity of thoughts comes from right views. What we see.

Man does unlimited work, his thoughts are unlimited. Have you ever thought about why we do things in life? We are doing it but why? One who recognizes this is successful. Why is it from your thoughts?

Thoughts take the form of behaviour. The reason for completing the task is the idea. Our thoughts calm us, no one calms us. We keep taking credit for ourselves through thoughts. Sometimes it happens that what makes us happy makes someone else sad. The quality of the ideas is great.

His style is very honest, he looks at thoughts from a true perspective. The excellence of his ideas is truly unique. Many changes happen through thoughts only. Our thoughts change with our environment.

There is a lot of truth in thoughts but they remain just thoughts. They preserve the inner clarity of man like some unique scene. Such thoughts flow with the highest ideology that blossoms in any fragrant state.

A positive environment can be created with the right change in thoughts. We remain unfamiliar with most ideas. One's inner thoughts can be detected through one's external actions, such as how much cement was used to build a road and what quality it was used for, can be detected through its external strength.

Similarly, one can know how strong one is from his/her thoughts. When we want to create a good environment then we have to make our ideas unique.

It begins a journey of ideas that will always encourage stronger thoughts. A process that inspires a right direction for a great purpose. The thoughts we give more importance to in life are the thoughts that create the future and present.

When the field of thoughts changes then every situation changes. The future is an excellent background of ideas that can be seen in practical actions. Man is dependent on thoughts. The infinite state of thoughts is visible in consciousness.

We can see where there is dirt and where there is cleanliness. Giving up limited thoughts and doing something big is the excellence and vast form of thoughts. There are many places in the world but there is a shortage of those thoughts which do not allow us to experience these places.

Our objectives are limited because our thoughts are limited. Unlimited thinking is the solution to various problems which gives the experience of peace in life. Only when the flow of thoughts is in the direction of the goal are the goals accomplished.

What is the real idea? The real idea is that which provides peace to your life and the lives of those around you. Many times in life we have to get entangled in such thoughts which waste our time and energy. Like someone said, catch a flying bird, who will benefit from it?

In life, the more accurate the thoughts are, the more important they will always be, which are related to truth. It will not be enough to remain immersed in unlimited thoughts, we should also have many goals like social, economic, educational.

Ultimately it can be said that when we take the right knowledge from the right resources and think right, then it is important to complete the big goal and big task which brings the possibility of development with joy and fragrance.

Goal Achievement Process

When we set a goal, it is accomplished by going through some steps. A goal is something that works like our task. There is a difference between task and goal, tasks are small while goals are big. The things we do every day are tasks. An example of a goal is to learn something over a period of time. Some work we do is a task.

Many tasks together make a big goal. We don't remember a task so much as we remember a goal. A goal is a process that we reach through tasks. A big goal is an extension of many tasks. The task is easy to complete. The tasks which we complete in a very short period of time are tasks.

To accomplish a goal, the first thing to do is to create the goal. When formulating goals, many parameters are prepared. The goal can be set only by looking at one's ability, capability and mentality. The goal should be one that requires complete hard work and if not achieved, there is a desire to work more hard.

Man's desire is also included in the goal. It is not right to change the goal if the goal is not achieved. When it seems that the goal will not be achieved then one more attempt can be made. If you feel like changing the goal then make another goal along with the goal but you have to work on both the goals.

The importance of goals in life is simply that your time and effort is not wasted. Even if you don't succeed, you still have the knowledge and experience. Waiting for the goal to be accomplished is futile because your concentration can get lost when you spend time waiting for the goal to be accomplished.

We are not able to do many important things, many important tasks while waiting for this. We know that the goal is being accomplished. Anything takes time to complete.

But neither too much nor too much work. Real people never set small goals but also do not pay attention to small problems. The difference is that they spend their remaining time in completing some other task or goal.

When they do not feel like working, they do not worry, nor are they afraid, nor are they nervous because they know that someone is supporting me, they know this very well. We learned how they score goals. We also have to set some target which is within our capability.

Their aim is the goal itself and not success. Setting goals is like living openly which only successful people do. Purpose is why we are aiming.

Nothing is free here. Your mentality also wants a goal. It is up to you to give him goals and remove his emptiness. There is a huge difference between desire and goal. Desire can be for anything. The aim is precise.

You are ready to move ahead in your ordinary life and pursue the goals and desires that make you the highest. Our life remains right and true in our own eyes due to the goal. Also try once for those goals which you want to achieve but are not achieving.

By being concerned with the goals of others, you set back your own goals. Always remember that your goal is greater than any of your circumstances. As long as the goal has a great beginning and a great end, it will keep you very happy.

You know you cannot do any work without food. Just as food is a resource for the body, similarly the goal is for the future. The process of achieving goals is a struggle. One who has linked goals to struggle will never succumb to any situation that may lead him astray.

Even vegetables don't taste good without spices, then how can life improve without goals? It is important to improve your life so that you can become someone's energy. Your cooperation may be sought for many tasks.

All the successful people do not see time, they see the goal. Have you ever fixed a time when your exam result comes that you will check your result only at this time? No, we remain curious, we keep waiting.

What about when someone is sick and says I will take medicine this time? This can be understood from many such examples in life. We have to understand the goal. How can we become efficient in achieving our goals?

We should not lack knowledge of any subject. Our energy is unlimited, our desires are unlimited, then how come our goals are so small. The aim of a goal in life is success.

You can aim to read a book that is full of stories. You may like to become something which field is of your interest. It takes hard work even to set a goal. You have to trust yourself, nature and the universe to help you.

Some people set goals based on their convenience. But if the choice is based on your knowledge, then your goal will be stronger because knowledge of any field is unlimited and experiences are also included in it.

What field do you love, do you like playing, do you want to become a teacher who can give his experience to many children to move in the right direction.

There is no point learning anything here. The more we set our goals, the closer we will get to freedom and success. There is no feeling of failure in this. People should be absolutely precise in this work.

Now you are ready to finish the process. Only as you move your feet away from the previous ladder will you be able to move forward. You will have to remove all those memories, all those resources that you have, only then will you be able to fully realize this process.

Remember all your actions that will make you feel the happiness you want in the future. You will have to remove all your useless things from yourself. No matter how close he is to you.

The more you have a feeling of sacrifice, the closer you will be to your goal. It is difficult to believe, only when you try it practically you will be able to believe it.

Don't think of collecting anything. This is the biggest obstacle to achieving the goal. Remember that what is yours today will belong to someone else in the future. If we aim at things that have happened or have been done in the past. Then your goal will be achieved but there will be no difference in it, it can get the status of copy.

Honesty should be dedicated to one's goal. The goal should be made but not with the aim of completion. In this you will create opportunities for many people. Meanwhile, due to greed, we consider this goal as our own. We have to give opportunity to those who have come to us with great hope. We must give them a chance. After achieving your goal, you can make yourself great by leaving it behind and helping others.

You may feel that we worked hard. Someone has said that cotton and oil have been burning here for centuries but people say that the lamp is burning. Very good, we will get everything by not getting disappointed and giving up.

Instead of looking at our own hard work, we should see the hard work of others and help them selflessly. One who makes life flow in the direction of light and takes it away.

❖

How to Live Peacefully?

The way to peace here is to listen to what those who kept writing even during the war had to say. Heartfelt salute...

My head is a jail
By Valeria Skvortsova, 24

My head - is a jail,
My room - is a jail too,
Messenger is my friend
And other social networks.

My enemy is everyone outside
And the air they breathe out.
I wasn't ready
For this fight alone.

I breathe in slowly
And count each passing breath.
My body is barren
But my soul hurts.

2.

We need to hurry up
Daria Chebotariova, 14

*We were told the war should end
But it keeps going from day to day.
And we forgot to smile and can't pretend,
We are surrounded by despair
And we keep waiting for someone to care.*

*The towns and villages are ruined at their core,
As are our hearts and souls.
We forget that every door
Has its own unique lock.*

*We still believe in a happy future,
Where we will live in harmony and peace.
We'll not forget those who have fallen,
That's why we need to hurry up.*

3.

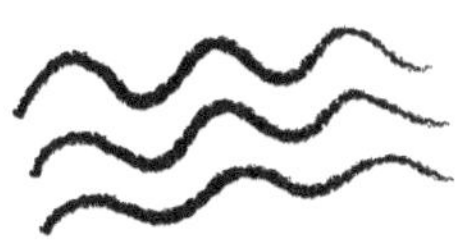

The puzzle
Viktoria Ponkrashkina, 16

I thought it was a dream,
but it happened to be real.
The torture of the war
And overwhelming fear.
I want it all to go away
Diffuse in shining sun
And troubles blown from our day
By friendly clouds, so far
I want people out of cellars
Living to the full
Not afraid of their jailers
Sleeping soundly.
I want to throw away all the pieces
From the puzzle of this cruel war
So children don't play with them
I want everyone to be happy and smile!

I believe in a happy Ukraine
And the new life beginning today!
I believe we can forget about war
It will be swept away from the shore.

4.

If peace comes
Hakim Karwan, 21

"Once again, every child shall have a pen in their hand. I was born and raised in conflict, but I hope to see my country free from conflict."

Life will be extremely beautiful when peace comes
Everyone will plant beautiful pine and palm trees
From these sprawling deserts we will make gardens again
We will return to our lands and sow green when peace comes

Once again, every child in my country will have a pen in their hand
We will take up pens and books, and become forgivers
We are tired of this war, we search for peace
We will gather together as brothers.

5.

I'm a child who loves peace
Sawsan Al-Shamiri, 10

"I hope that all the pigeons and the olive trees grow up and we will be in peace... I hope the whole world will be filled with peace."

I am a child who loves peace
I have always believed in peace
Until I saw something on TV,
Something not expected at all.

I saw on the screen war and destruction
I saw children sleeping in tents
They lost the embrace and protection of their parents
I saw children who are as skinny as ghosts
I saw schools and parks empty of children.

I cried from what I saw and went to the source of love, my father
I asked him: Where did peace go?
Where are schools and parks?
Where is medicine and where is food?

6.

The Youth are...
Hiba Mohamed Hassan, 19

The Youth are a pillar
And a national symbol
They are a ray of light
And the future of the whole country
Without them
It means
A house without foundation
And with no entry point (door)
My point is
They can create peace
And can shape the future
Our beautiful land
They can illuminate it
They are Immutable flowers
That can benefit the people

Conclusion-

The huge amount of words diverts the right decisions of life from the flow. Life is dynamic. We blame it on reasons that are not ours. What is ours takes time to complete. We have created such a society that it is difficult to change. We are told to do this and no one motivates us to do the right thing in the right direction. If we do, then we are insulted.

Despite all the difficulties, some people shine so much that they always come forward and become violent when the people around them do harm to us. It is easy to change society. Not trying to change it is the effort. Unless he stumbles, he will not be able to understand it. It says go like this, do like this. Whenever you say something right, it tries to suppress it.

We need an organization where there is neither discrimination nor ignorance.

Those who have something shining inside them help others to shine too but should we praise them? No, not at all. To stay at such places is to bargain with your freedom, to compromise.

The goal of life is freedom. We have to strive for freedom with courage.

There are some fools who leave behind their goals and pursue us. They do not understand what is right and what is wrong. They only see their own benefit. Greed is clearly visible in their eyes. Trust should be given very thoughtfully. Are people making you their slave by speaking good words to you? It has become easy to cheat in the name of relationship.

Man should have extended his helping hand but he does not want to correct the situation. There is neither any juice nor any fragrance in his life. It is foolish to ignore what is visible.

If ever there is a need to run away then it is right to run away because living in a negative environment will make you negative.

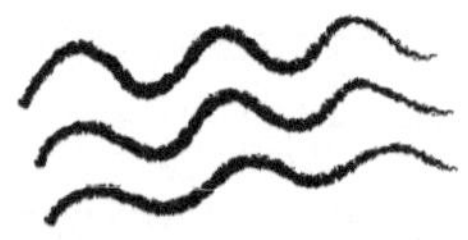